Expressions of the Human Spirit

by Jackie Levin

AbleNet®, Inc., Minneapolis, Minnesota

AbleNet, Inc.
1081 Tenth Ave. S.E.
Minneapolis, MN 55414-1312
1-800-322-0956 US & Canada
1-612-379-0956 US & Global

ISBN 0-9666667-0-4

For my father....

Acknowledgements

Special thanks to the following individuals:
Cheryl Volkman...for your belief in the vision and commitment to making it happen
Janelle Weyek...for your professional expertise and guidance
Theresa Curran...for your support in managing the details
Shirley Thompson...for your time and assistance
Pam Schoffner...for your edits and refinements that made a difference
Sandy Nelson...for your advice and encouragement
John Haines...for your creativity and ability to reflect the depth of this message

...and my deepest gratitude to Peggy Locke...for your wisdom and the incredible synergy we continue to create

Introduction

I vividly remember beginning my first "real" job when I completed college nearly 22 years ago and entered a segregated school for almost 200 secondary age students with disabilities. As a novice speech and language pathologist with little clinical practice serving such a population, I was awed and humbled by the experience.

My initial lack of knowledge, confidence and perceived abilities left me seriously considering whether it was I—rather than my students—who had the greater disability in that environment. I completed my first year with an incredible appreciation for the diversity in the abilities of human beings.

As the years progressed, our student population became even more challenged until my entire caseload consisted of learners with the most severe/profound cognitive and physical disabilities. Once again I was humbled, and once again my appreciation for the term "differing abilities" deepened.

Through my tenure, one of my most valuable insights was recognizing the importance of subtle human behavior...a glance of recognition when someone familiar entered the room, a gesture toward a toy that might indicate a preference or a grimace that really meant "I'm so happy you're here.

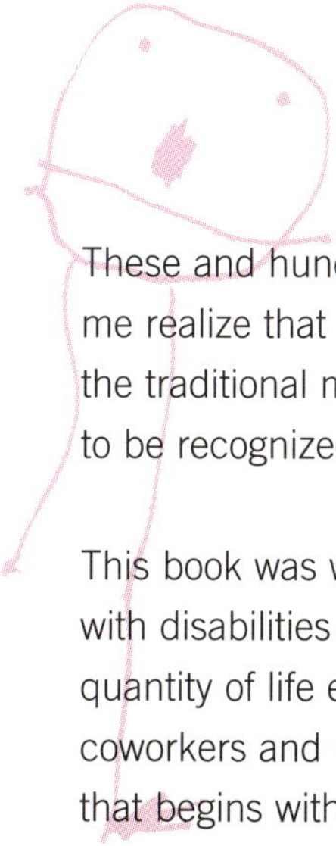

believe

These and hundreds of other verbal and nonverbal "communications" helped me realize that although the "language" of my students was different from the traditional mode, the purpose and intent were the same...to have friends, to be recognized, to have fun, to be comforted, to learn.

This book was written with the primary purpose of being a "voice" of people with disabilities everywhere who desire and deserve the same quality and quantity of life experiences as their non-disabled peers, family members, coworkers and neighbors. To this end, the rest of us have a significant role that begins with a very simple step...to listen and consider the unspoken messages of the many who have so much to tell us.

Perhaps by taking time to read, consider and "hear" these messages, you may develop a deeper appreciation for what may also be important in your own life. I invite you to share in the universal message that exists in *Expressions of the Human Spirit* and embrace the belief that we are all much more alike than we are different.

Jackie Levin

If life is an Adventure...

let me Discover

the magic in my journey.

If seeing is **B**elieving.....

see my Abilities and

know I too can make a difference!

If Creativity is an inherent gift in everyone....

help me reveal my own

creative Talents!

If Discipline builds competence

and confidence...

expect me to Practice

new skills every day!

If choices are the key to self-**E**mpowerment...

let me **Choose** so I

may learn to trust myself!

If true **F**riends keep the spirit alive...

surround me with opportunities to make

life-sustaining Connections!

If Greatness is measured by

who we are, not what we do...

find a way for me to

Stand in my own light!

If Happiness comes to those

who can be present in the moment...

take time Now to

involve me in what's happening!

If Intelligence has many faces...

see my gifts and recognize

how "Smart" I am!

If Joy is the expression of a smiling heart...

give my heart a

reason to Laugh!

If **K**indness is the greatest medicine

there is...

accept my **C**ompassion

so you may be soothed!

If Learning awakens a sleeping mind...

teach me so my eyes

may Open!

If **M**emories are treasures of the heart...

provide me with

Experiences to remember!

If Nature is a source of unlimited pleasure...

show me the Wonders

of earth's natural beauty!

If an **O**pen door leads to greater opportunity...

remove the **B**arriers

so I can be on my way!

If life is full of simple Pleasures...

help me experience the

Joy of the simple things!

If Questions are the key to discovery...

encourage me to ask so I

may find my own Answers!

If **R**esponsibility is a priviledge of growing up...

allow me to **Participate**

in the rites of passage!

If Success is measured by our personal bests...

let me experience pride in my

own Accomplishments!

If **T**ogether we're better...

involve me in activities so I too can

make a Contribution!

If **U**nderstanding can occur at many levels...

recognize the unique ways

I do Comprehend!

If Variety is the spice of life...

fill my world with the richness

of diversity!

If the spirit seeks a place of **W**onder...

bring me to the

Excitement!

If eXpressions of the human spirit are a window to the soul...

listen closely to

what I have to "say!"

If people Yearn to speak their truth...

provide me with a

Voice so I can be heard!

If experiencing real fun creates a **Z**est

for life...

then never forget, I am

just like Everyone else!

About the Author

Jackie Levin is Vice President of Product Development and co-founder of AbleNet, Inc. Her background as a speech language pathologist and coordinator of a simple technology program for a large special education school district in Minnesota was the catalyst for developing product concepts and education materials that would open new opportunities and experiences for individuals with severe disabilities. Ms. Levin was inspired by her belief that we all have gifts to share and can change the course of our lives and those around us through the experiences and opportunities we create.

About AbleNet

Believing that people with severe disabilities are capable and contributing members of every family, school and community, AbleNet took root in 1985 as a not-for-profit designer and manufacturer of simple-to-use technology. Since the company became a for-profit entity in 1990, two percent of annual pre-tax earnings have been prioritized for corporate giving. Publishing *Expressions of the Human Spirit* will increase that percentage; the majority of profits will be donated to programs that enrich lives and broaden the possibilities for every generation.

It is our hope and passion that *Expressions of the Human Spirit* will help people recognize the potential of persons with severe disabilities and inspire them to provide the opportunities necessary for each individual to reach his or her full potential.